Published by Creative Education
123 South Broad Street, Mankato, Minnesota 56001
Creative Education is an imprint of The Creative Company

Designed by Stephanie Blumenthal
Production Design by The Design Lab
Editorial Assistance by Rosemary Wallner

Photos by: AP/Wide World Photos, Archive Photos, Camera Press,
DMI Photos, Everett Collection, Globe Photos, Photofest, Shooting Star,
Retna Ltd., Rex USA Ltd.

Library of Congress Cataloging-in-Publication Data

Guilfoyle, Peg, 1950–
Oprah Winfrey / by Peg Guilfoyle
p. cm. (Ovations)
Summary: A biography of the performer and talk show host, discussing her
childhood of neglect and her rise to the top of the entertainment world.
ISBN 0-88682-941-0

1. Winfrey, Oprah—Juvenile literature. 2. Television personalities—United
States—Biography—Juvenile literature. 3. Motion picture actors and
actresses—United States—Biography—Juvenile literature. [1. Winfrey, Oprah.
2. Television personalities. 3. Actors and actresses. 4. Afro-Americans—Biography. 5. Women—Biography] I. Title. II. Series: Ovations (Mankato, Minn.)

PN1992.4.W56G85   1999
791.45'028'092—dc21   98-4214
(B)

First edition

2   4   6   8   9   7   5   3   1

OPRAH

WINFREY

BY PEG GUILFOYLE

Creative ✿ Education

REFLECTIONS

At first glance, Oprah Winfrey is glamorous. She lives in a mansion and has her own chef and trainer. She wears designer clothes, stars in movies, and is close friends with many famous people. She has been among the highest-paid performers since the late 1980s. In 1996 her earnings were estimated at $171 million. Forbes magazine tallies up Oprah's total worth at $550 million. This total is based on the syndication value of her TV shows and film deal with ABC/Disney.

But every day on "The Oprah Winfrey Show," her audience sees a different side of the talk show star. Like a girlfriend, sister, or a mentor, Oprah is with us every day. Her shows are filled with engaging people with interesting things to say. She is funny, candid, eager to listen, and eager to

talk—whatever the topic. After years of public discussion, five days a week, about everything from celebrity lifestyles to weight control, everybody knows Oprah. Her brilliant smile and open, eager expression welcome people into the conversation. Her guests, whether average people or superstars, watch her admiringly while she shapes her show to suit herself and her audience.

Oprah is a woman in her element and in her prime. She is powerful, confident, at ease with herself, successful, and she seems determined to use her power to benefit others. Her good works make her a role model for us all. But her life has not always been like this. Born out of wedlock, she had a tough childhood and got into lots of trouble. She was mistreated and got into bad relationships with boys, and later, with men. Her mother once tried to get her admitted into reform school. Oprah still struggles every day with a weight problem. How do we know these things? Because she has told us, the way a good friend would.

Although Oprah's work involves frequent interviews with such recognizable personalities as Hillary Clinton, above, her off-camera interests are very down-to-earth.

EVOLUTION

Oprah was born on January 29, 1954, in Kosciusko, Mississippi. (Oprah is an accidental misspelling of the biblical name Orpah.) Her parents were not married, and her father, Vernon Winfrey, did not know about her birth until afterward. While he was serving in the Army, he got a letter from eighteen-year-old Vernita Lee announcing the birth of a girl, with a simple note attached that said, "Send clothes." Shortly after Oprah's birth, Vernita left the baby with Vernon's mother and moved north to Milwaukee, Wisconsin, in search of a better job. For six years Oprah was raised by her grandmother, whom she called Momma.

Oprah's grandmother, Hattie Mae, was strict. Oprah sometimes had to cut a springy stick for her own whipping. Hattie Mae had strong opinions about education, too. She

tutored her granddaughter so that she could do arithmetic, read, and write by age three.

At age six, Oprah was sent to live with Vernita, who worked as a maid in Milwaukee. This began a series of moves across the country between her parents. At age eight, Oprah moved down to Nashville to live with her father and his wife Velma; she returned to her mother a few years later but attended high school and college in Nashville.

Oprah had a lot of trouble during her junior high years, made worse by the unstable atmosphere in her mother's home. Oprah was sexually abused by an older cousin and, later, by other boys and men. "I didn't tell anybody about it because I thought I would be blamed for it. I remember blaming myself for it, thinking something must be wrong with me," she recalled years later.

Her reading habit caught the attention of a teacher, who recognized Oprah's exceptional intelligence. "Mr. Abrams was one of those great teachers who had the ability to make you believe in yourself," she said. He arranged a scholarship to an all-white school in a Milwaukee suburb. It was an enormous change for the thirteen-year-old; she was the only black out of 2,000 students.

Oprah's education, her parents, Vernita and Vernon, opposite top, and her religious beliefs, fostered at her family church in Kosciusko, Mississippi, opposite bottom, helped stabilize Oprah's life during her turbulent teenage years.

At the new school, Oprah did well in her classes and became popular, but she also became frustrated. Every day she rode the local bus from her poor, inner-city neighborhood to the prosperous white suburb. The only other blacks making that trip were the maids who worked in her classmates' homes. After school, "It was like going back to Cinderella's house from the castle every night," she said later. Like anyone else, she wanted the security of the life she saw in school and in her classmates' homes.

Confused and angry, she began to get into trouble. She lied and stole from her mother and stayed out late. When she was fourteen, she ran away from home for a week. Eventually, she arrived back home, but her mother had had enough. Vernita wanted her daughter admitted to a home for troubled teens.

"I remember going to the interview process, where they treat you like you're already a known convict. . . . I knew that I was a smart person. I knew I wasn't a bad person, and I remember thinking: 'How did this happen? How did I get here?'"

Fortunately for Oprah, the home was full. Vernita called the girl's father in Nashville. Vernon drove to Milwaukee and picked up his daughter, who had not lived with him in eight years. Shortly after their return to Nashville, Oprah had a baby. She has apparently never been sure who the father was; the baby lived only a short while.

On the Path

"I got sent to live with my father so that [he] could straighten me out, and that he did," Oprah said.

Her father and stepmother were loving but strict. C's on a report card were not good enough; tight clothing was not acceptable; she had a nightly curfew.

Oprah flourished in Nashville. Encouraged to read, she began to read everything. She especially connected with Maya Angelou's autobiography titled *I Know Why the Caged Bird Sings*. Angelou too had been shuttled between parents and had been raped and traumatized. Years later, the two women be- came close friends.

At East Nashville High, Oprah was the student council president, was voted Most Popular, and dated the Most Popular boy. She gave speeches and dramatic recitations, including representations of black women such as Sojourner Truth and Harriet Tubman. Oprah was invited to the White House Council on Youth and, at age sixteen, traveled to Los Angeles to give one of her speeches. While there, she visited Mann's Chinese Theatre and ran her hands over the sidewalk where famous people's handprints are impressed. Returning home, she told her father she planned to be famous, too.

Oprah's personality and talents shone in high school, but she also had lucky breaks. For a March of Dimes Walk-a-Thon, she persuaded a local disc jockey to sponsor her. When she went to collect the money, he liked her voice. The station needed minority broadcasters and wanted more female voices. Oprah was hired to read news on weekends and after school, a job that lasted into her first year of college.

She also began to win beauty contests. In 1971, she was the first black woman to win the Miss Fire Prevention contest, charming the judges

Oprah's love for literature, inspired in part by her mentor, poet Maya Angelou, above, makes her a dynamic spokeswoman on the benefits of reading and learning.

while answering a standard contest question. Flashing a brilliant smile Oprah answered, "If I had a million dollars . . . I'd be a spending fool!"

Oprah later was crowned Miss Black Nashville and then Miss Black Tennessee. In an Elks Club contest, she won a four-year scholarship to Tennessee State University.

In college, Oprah continued landing important jobs at a young age. In 1973, she was hired as the co-anchor on the newscasts of WTVF in Nashville, moving from radio to television. She was the first woman, and the first black, to hold the job, working there for three years.

ROUGHER WATERS

In 1976, at the age of twenty-two, Oprah moved to a larger station. WJZ-TV in Baltimore, Ohio, was expanding its evening newscast and wanted a co-anchor. The fact that Oprah was black, and a woman, was again an advantage. By taking the job, she moved for the first time away from her family.

Her time in Baltimore began badly. She did not get along well with her co-anchor, and she had difficulty reading the news. Reporting on tragedies like house fires and murders was difficult for Oprah. "It was not good for a news reporter to be out covering a fire and crying with a woman who has lost her home," she said. "How do you not worry about a woman who has lost all seven children and everything she's owned in a fire? How do you not cry about that?"

After nine months, WJZ replaced Oprah as news anchor. Holding a six-year contract, the station had to give her something to do. "They came to me and said, 'Your eyes are too far apart, your nose is too wide, your chin is too long, and you need to do something about it.' So they sent me to New York, to a chi-chi poo-poo, lah-de-dah salon—the kind that serves you wine so when you leave it doesn't matter what you look like." The permanent they gave her hair burned her scalp, but she didn't complain. A week later, all of Oprah's hair fell out. "You learn a lot about yourself when you are black and bald," she said.

It was a low point in her career, tough even for such a strong and determined personality.

ONWARD AND UPWARD

The management of the Baltimore TV station decided to produce a local talk show and let Oprah cohost. When her job was to talk with people, her skills and strong personality worked together.

Throughout her well-documented struggles with weight, Oprah has forged a television career decorated with dozens of Emmy Awards.

"I said to myself, 'This is what I should be doing,'" she recalled. "It's like breathing." Before long, the show, "People Are Talking," had more Baltimore viewers than its competition.

Oprah stayed with "People Are Talking" for three years, developing a large following. Her personal life was not going so well, however. She fell in love with a man who was not kind to her. The former beauty queen also gained weight and began a lifelong struggle with dieting and food. Her mostly female audience loved her even when she was heavy; after all, many women worry about their weight. It made them feel that she was in some ways just like they were.

In 1983, one of the "People Are Talking" producers took a new job at a WLS-TV morning talk show called "A.M. Chicago." Needing a new host, the producer suggested auditioning Oprah. The station manager's reaction to Oprah's audition was, "Holy smokes. This is something." He said, "I had looked at tapes for years, but never had I seen anything like Oprah. She is a unique personality. So up. So effervescent. So television. So spontaneous and unrehearsed. She was not like anyone else on the tube."

Oprah was a huge hit in Chicago, where her style, enthusiasm, and genuine interest in people had her show beating the competition in less

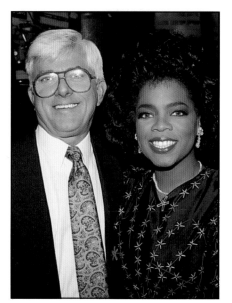

Oprah has proven her skills as an actress in such movies as Before Women Had Wings, opposite bottom, and The Color Purple, opposite top, a film directed by Steven Spielberg, bottom. Like former Chicago talk show host Phil Donahue, middle, Oprah has also gathered a huge television following.

than a year. "There aren't a lot of black people in Chicago media," said the station manager. "It was like you could hear TVs clicking on [to Oprah] all over the city."

Time magazine said, "Guests with sad stories to tell are apt to rouse a tear in Oprah's eye. . . . They, in turn, often find themselves revealing things they would not imagine telling anyone, much less a national TV audience. It is the talk show as group-therapy session."

Oprah was thrilled with her success but continued to struggle with her eating habits and her weight. "I thought I was handling the stress just fine. The show was going well. I was doing great. Everyone told me how easy I made it look. But underneath I was terrified. So at night I'd sit up alone in my room at the Knickerbocker Hotel and order French onion soup by the gallon. 'Oh, and could you fry up a cheese sandwich to go with that?' That's how I was handling things."

Four-time Academy Award–winner Quincy Jones happened to tune in while in town on business. Jones was co-producing and writing the score for a new movie based on Alice Walker's book *The Color Purple.* Over

breakfast in the hotel, he flipped through the channels and landed on Oprah's show. There he knew he had found the right person to play the character of Sofia.

Oprah took time off from her talk show to make the film, which starred Whoopi Goldberg and was directed by Steven Spielberg. The film was nominated for eleven Academy Awards, including Best Picture, and Oprah was nominated as Best Supporting Actress. She did not win nor did *The Color Purple*. "It was the worst night of my life," remembered Oprah. "I could not go through the night pretending that it was okay that *Color Purple* did not win an Oscar. . . . I was stunned."

At just about the same time she was finishing *The Color Purple*, Oprah made a deal with the TV station that gave her control of her show, now renamed "The Oprah Winfrey Show." Soon it was syndicated and shown on 180 stations. Her company, Harpo Productions—for "Oprah" spelled backwards—began producing the daily talk show and other TV shows and films.

Oprah's infectious energy always shines through, whether she's on the set of a film such as Women of Brewster Place, *above, or celebrating her weight loss with a national television audience.*

Oprah has reaped huge rewards from her talents and determination. She is one of the country's most admired women and has received many awards. By 1998, "The Oprah Winfrey Show" had been honored with thirty Emmys; she had been named the Broadcaster of the Year; and she had received four image awards from the NAACP. Her interest in other TV projects and in films continued. Many acting and producing projects reflect her lifelong interest in children and in helping people better themselves.

At various times, often in response to guests with similar problems, she has discussed her own abuse as a child, her family, her use of cocaine in the 1970s, and her struggles with self-esteem and weight control. These revelations seem to deepen her connection with the audience. She often talks about the importance of overcoming adversity.

Over the years, Oprah has found good causes to support. In 1987, she established a series of scholarships in her father's name at Tennessee State University. She has also donated two million dollars to establish the Oprah Winfrey Endowment Scholarship Fund at Morehouse College in Atlanta.

She worked for the passage of the National Child Protection Act in 1994—sometimes called The Oprah Bill—which created a national data bank of convicted child abusers.

Helping others is an area her longtime boyfriend, Stedman Graham, knows well. An executive of SGA, Inc., Graham Gregory Bozell, Inc., and Kemper Golf Management, he is also the founder of Athletes Against Drugs, a nonprofit organization dedicated to eradicating drug use among America's youths. The author of *You Can Make It Happen*, a motivational book, he promotes education and people helping themselves. "I don't want to be somebody who just says, 'OK, here is some money,'" he said. "I want to give back through teaching 'how' to get it done."

The core of Oprah's success has been her daily talk show, seen by millions of viewers, and in this work too, she tries to be a positive influence. When "The Oprah Winfrey Show" and the other talk shows first began, they often chose shocking topics, hoping for high ratings. The intense competition caused some shows to be of questionable value. In 1994, Oprah announced that she would try to make better choices for her show. She said:

With the constant support of her boyfriend Stedman Graham, middle, and the encouragement of such friends as film and music producer Quincy Jones, top, Oprah has become a powerful screen presence. Her acting credits include a leading role in Beloved, opposite top, a 1998 film by Jonathan Demme, opposite bottom.

"We really ought to ask ourselves, 'Do we want our children to spend hours viewing the images we're putting on the tube these days? Do we want our children influenced by visions of death and destruction, carnage and car crashes, sex and scandals?'

"Sure, we can ease our consciences by telling ourselves that all of this devastation and ugliness falls under the heading of news, of the public's right, need, and desire to know. But shouldn't we also ask this: 'What effect are these images having on our children, and do they really give today's youth a realistic picture of our world?'"

Oprah's ratings dropped for a time but then rebounded. The president of her production house said, "There were particular shows in the early years we weren't too proud of, but now 'The Oprah Winfrey Show' stands out in the midst of all the spectacle talk shows that are confrontational, exploitative, and disgusting."

In 1996, in an effort to share her love of reading with her immense audience, Oprah started an on-air book club, asking her viewers to read a book that would be discussed on a future show. Those books have become best-sellers. Her interest in fitness and health issues led to the publication of a cookbook by her then-personal chef Rosie Daley, and, in 1996, to *Make the Connection: Ten Steps to a Better Body—and a Better Life*.

In 1997 and 1998, she was involved in a lawsuit in Texas, where she was sued by the cattle industry as a result of a show that discussed the possible health dangers of eating beef. She won, claiming a victory on behalf of free speech.

In 1998, Oprah signed up for two more years of "The Oprah Winfrey Show" for a reported $130 million. She also announced a commitment to make six TV movies for ABC and to star in a film version of Toni Morrison's Pulitzer Prize–winning novel, *Beloved*.

Throughout her career, many books and articles have been written about Oprah, her TV show, and her life. But Oprah herself has not yet written her autobiography, nor has she authorized anyone to write one. Sometimes the stories about her life seem incredible; sometimes other people don't agree with her version of the truth. Writing things down might clear up some details, but Oprah's medium is talk, and for the most part, that is how we learn about the life of this caring, successful woman.

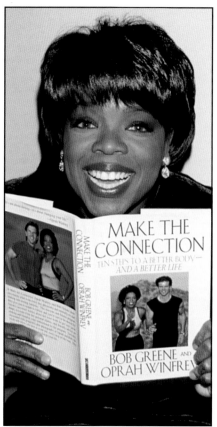

Emphasizing the benefits of reading through her on-air book club and her own book, Oprah has spread her passion for literature with the same enthusiasm that has driven her television and film success.

V O I C E S

O N   S U C C E S S :

"We embrace Oprah with open arms."

An Amarillo, Texas, fan,
during the beef trial

"I've been successful all these years
because I do my show with the people
in mind, not for the corporations or
their money."

Oprah Winfrey,
during the beef trial

"What I know is that God, nature, the
Spirit, the universe, whatever title you
wish to give him—or her—is always try-
ing to help each one of us to be the
best and do the best that we can."

Oprah Winfrey

"If she stays popular and with the show, [Oprah] Winfrey is well on her way to becoming America's first black billionaire."

Robert La Franco and Josh McHugh, in Forbes

Oprah's ten commandments for a successful life:

1. Don't live your life to please other people.
2. Don't depend on externals to help you get ahead.
3. Strive for the greatest possible harmony and compassion in your business and your life.
4. Get rid of all the back-stabbers around you.
5. Be nice, not catty.
6. Get rid of your addictions.
7. Surround yourself with people who are as good or better than you are.
8. If you're in it to make money, forget it.
9. Never give up your power to another person.
10. Don't give up.

◯N HER BOOK CLUB:

"On a really good day, [Oprah Winfrey] sends more people to bookstores than the morning news programs, the other talk shows, the evening magazines, radio shows, print reviews, and feature articles rolled into one."

NY Times Book Review

"I've always loved books. My idea is to reintroduce reading to people who've forgotten it exists."

Oprah Winfrey

"I was so surprised that it really was Oprah [calling to tell me that my novel *The Deep End of the Ocean* was the initial recommendation of her Book Club], because there is not much of a tradition of writers on talk shows." As her book rose past the big names on the New York Times fiction best-seller list, "I felt I was having an out-of-body experience."

Jacqueline Mitchard, author

"Books showed me there were possibilities in life, that there were actually people like me living in a world I could not only aspire to but attain. Reading gave me hope. For me it was the open door."

Oprah Winfrey

Oprah's devotion to quality, reputable television broadcasting is rivaled only by her interest in the literary accomplishments of such authors as Jacqueline Mitchard, middle, and the company of Stedman, bottom.

ON HER SHOW:

"Oprah opened up a lot of new windows because [women] could empathize with her."

> *Maury Povich,*
> *fellow talk show host*

"[Oprah is] a real person in the fake world of TV."

> *Marvin Kitman,*
> Newsday *columnist*

"Oprah is probably the greatest media influence on the adult population. She is almost a religion."

> *writer Fran Lebowitz,*
> *in* Time *magazine*

SUPPORTING WOMEN:

"American women love Oprah Winfrey, and Oprah loves them back."

> *Debra Dickerson,*
> *in* U.S. News and World Report

"The greatest responsibility I feel is to my Creator, and what I try to fulfill for myself is to honor the creation. The fact that I was created a black woman in this lifetime, everything in my life is built around honoring that. I feel a sense of reverence to that. I hold it sacred. And so I am always asking the question, 'What do I owe in service having been created a black woman?'"

> *Oprah Winfrey*

Much of Oprah's public life involves working and mingling with such high-profile celebrities as pop star Michael Jackson, opposite, Barbara Walters, middle, and supermodel Cindy Crawford, bottom.

"Though not a religious person in the traditional sense, Oprah is nonetheless extremely spiritual. She says she's never missed a day of prayer and meditation in her entire life. She even refers to her show as 'my ministry.'"

Redbook Magazine

O N H E R R E L A T I O N S H I P S :

"Every time they try to make fun of me they really do women an injustice. Women have a difficult time finding anybody that will accept the fact that they make more money, that they may have a better position, and that they're in the limelight."

Stedman Graham talking about his relationship with Oprah and the fact that she makes more money than he does

"Who wouldn't want to be her best friend?"

Gayle King, Oprah's best friend

"Gayle [King] is the reason I don't need therapy."

Oprah Winfrey, on her best friend

Oprah's beliefs and way of life—supported and inspired by Maya Angelou, top, best friend Gayle King, bottom, and partner Stedman—make her a strong woman and a role model for many people.

ON HER SELF-IMAGE:

"She's a different person now. The most important thing is that she's satisfied with herself."

Stedman Graham,
Oprah's boyfriend

"I don't believe that it's for everybody to be a size 8 or even a 12. I think you need to be where you physically feel the best for you."

Oprah Winfrey

ON HER TEMPTATIONS:

"If you're angry, be angry and deal with it. Don't go eat a bag of Ruffles."

Oprah Winfrey

"I was never a Ding Dongs, Twinkies girl. I'm into salty, crunchy foods. Caramel and cheese popcorn send me over the edge."

Oprah Winfrey

"For me, food was comfort, pleasure, love, a friend, everything. [Now] I consciously work every day at not letting food be a substitute for my emotions."

Oprah Winfrey

Having overcome many struggles through determination, a commitment to a healthy lifestyle, and the help of those close to her, Oprah is a celebrity that millions of fans consider a friend.

OVATIONS